Water is Life!

I0161748

Iyako Nipy Pimatisiwin!

By Dhedra Dumas

Illustrated by Robin Ducharme Sr.

DEDICATION

I would like to dedicate this book to my children, Robin Ducharme Jr. and Darley Ducharme.

ACKNOWLEDGMENTS

THANK YOU TO EVELYN RAVEN FOR THE CREE TRANSLATION. ROBIN DUCHARME SR. FOR THE ART WORK. I ALSO WOULD LIKE TO THANK JANICE SETO AND RALPH CARIBOU. THANK YOU ALL VERY MUCH AND KEEP UP THE GOOD JOB.

WATER
IS
Life
Iyako Nipiy
Pimatisiwin

Water is life, water gives life. Water must be treated with respect.

Nipiy ohci Kapimatisiyahk. Nipy kapi kistithitamok.

Water helps plants grow.
Water helps food grow.

Nipiy ohci kahkithaw kisti
kana kapimatisimakak.

Water helps with everyone's favorite fruit. Bananas, apples, blueberries, and strawberries.

Nipiy ohci minsa nihtawikinaw nanatohk minsa askih okistikana.

Water helps trees grow, trees gives us fresh air.

Nipiy ohci sihtak nihtawikiwak yikohtah ohci mitho kikwan ohcimakan.

Water even supplies hydro-electricity. From strong flowing water falls.

Nipiy ohci pithisiwisokiw ka-ohcimakak misi pawistikwa kisiciwana misiwi.

Always use water wisely, don't waste water.

Kapi kwask nipiy apacihtatan.

Any living human or animal even insects need water to survive. Some animals live in water. Fish, otters, beavers.

Kahkihthaw itiniwak, pisikiwak, mina mancosak nipiy pimatcihikwak. Kinosiwak, nikikwak, amiskwak nipiy pimatcihikwak.

Birds swim, eat and take breaks when they migrate on water.

Kapimahakaw nipinasak nipiyhik kipihciwak, micisowak, minihkwiwak.

Water is always flowing, you never step in the same water twice.

Kapi pimitciwan nipiy, mwac niswaw katahkoskatin.

Human bodies are made mostly of water. This is why you must stay hydrated.

Ethiniwak nipiyihk ohciwak. Nipiy piko taminihkwiyan kapimatisin.

Remember not all water is drinkable. Most of Mother earth is ocean.

Kikawinaw Askiy ayaw mihciht misinipiyak.
Mwac atiht ki kokiminihkanaw.

Which is why we must keep our
fresh water, Fresh.

Piko tahmanahcihtayahk nipiy
ota askihk.

Water also provides recreational activities. You can swim during the summer.

Kapi nipin, awasisak pakasimowak kipimiskananaw, kikwaskwipicikanan kanipihk minsa kapipohk.

During winter you can ice skate, on frozen water, rivers, lakes, ponds, brooks are frozen solid.

Kakisoskatahin misiwi kapipohk, sakahikanihk, sipihak, sakahikanisisa ahkwatinaw misiwi.

Water helps natural medicine grow, such as rat root and natural mint.

Maskihkiya, wihkis, wihkaskwa nipihk nihtawikinwa.

When rain falls those are droplets of water falling to help vegetation.

Oma kakimiwahk mithokinwah askihk kistikana.

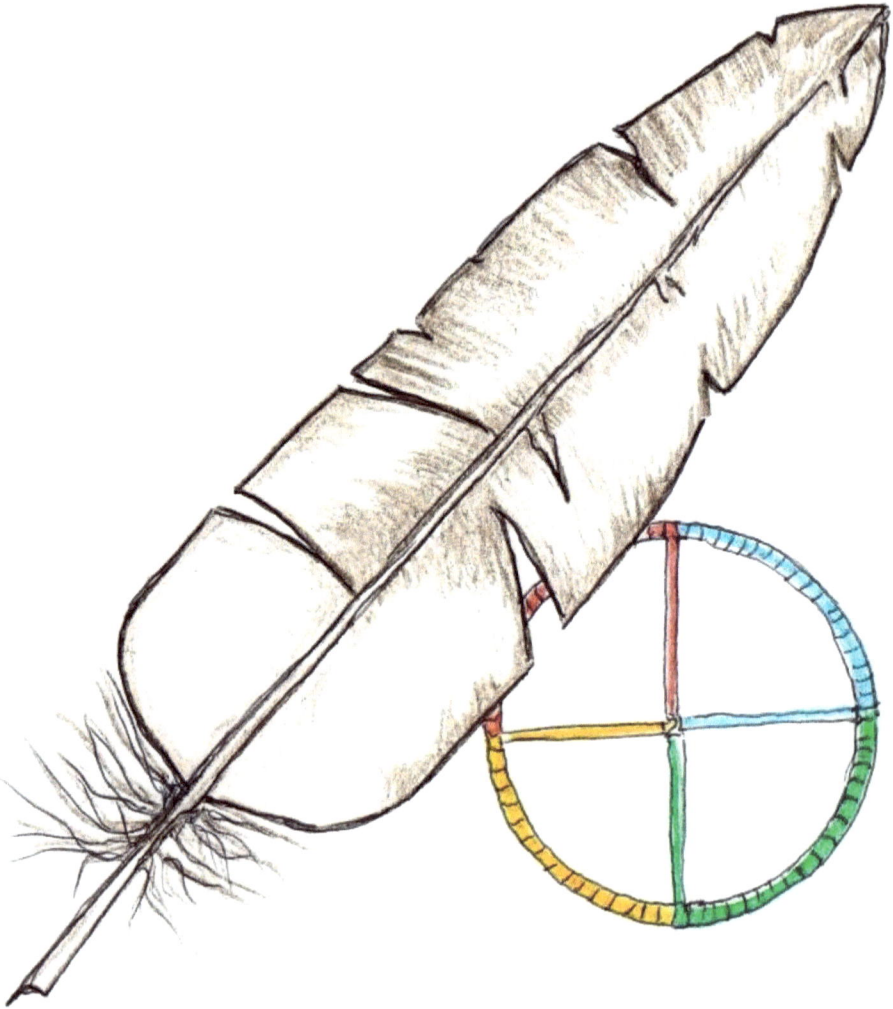

Respect water, don't waste it because water is Life.

Kisithitamok kapi nipiy, iyako kapimatcihikoyahk ota asihk. Mwac kikwan kitah pimatisimakan ikanipiy itakwakih.

This book is about the importance of water and why it is special.

ABOUT THE AUTHOR

SHE GREW UP AT A SMALL NORTHERN MANITOBA RESERVE. SHE WAS TAUGHT THE IMPORTANCE OF WATER GROWING UP. NOW I AM PASSING ON MY KNOWLEDGE TO THE NEXT GENERATION.

www.ingramcontent.com/pod-product-compliance
Lightning Source LLC
Chambersburg PA
CBHW041801040426
42448CB00001B/7